WALTER T. BERGEN SCHOOL
BLOOMINGDALE, NEW JERSEY

A DAY THAT MADE HISTORY

THE LAST DAY
IN SAIGON

John Griffiths

Dryad Press Limited / David & Charles Inc.

Contents

THE EVENTS

THE INVESTIGATION

Acknowledgments

The author and publishers thank the following for their kind permission to reproduce copyright illustrations: Britain Vietnam Association, pages 19, 32, 45, 51, 53, 54; Camera Press Ltd, pages 15, 23, 41, 47, 50, 52; Embassy of the Socialist Republic of Vietnam, pages 8, 10, 29, 34, 37, 46, 48, 57; Popperfoto, pages 9, 13, 16, 27, 36, 40, 55. The cartoon on page 61 is by Nuez. The stamps on pages 22 and 49 are reproduced courtesy of COPREFIL. The map on page 5 was drawn by R.F. Brien. The photographs on page 14 are from the author's collection. The poster on the front cover was designed by the Cuban designer Mederos for OSPAAL.

Nicholas Griffiths carried out the documentary and picture research for this book and gave the author invaluable guidance. It is his book as much as the author's. Special thanks also to Elaine Fuller and Morton Sobell and to the Strand Bookshop, New York.

The "Day that Made History" series was devised by Nathaniel Harris.

© John Griffiths 1986. First published 1986.
Typeset by Tek-Art Ltd, Kent, and printed in Great Britain by R.J. Acford, Chichester, Sussex for the publishers, Dryad Press Limited, 8 Cavendish Square, London W1M 0AJ
Published in the USA by: David & Charles Inc., North Pomfret, Vermont 05053
ISBN 0 8521 9671 7

THE
EVENTS

"Get those Marines out!"

30th April, 1975

In Washington D.C. Henry Kissinger, the US Secretary of State, triumphantly announced to the press that all Americans had been evacuated from Saigon, which was encircled by advancing North Vietnamese troops. Before the press conference ended, at just after 4 p.m., an assistant handed him a note: there were still US Marines in the American Embassy in Saigon. Kissinger did not pass on this piece of information to the press, but as soon as the conference ended he raced to his office. "Get those Marines out!" he raged. Heads would roll if a single Marine were killed.

The Marines were the last remaining Americans in Saigon. Their task had been to guard the US Embassy whilst Americans, together with certain South Vietnamese, were evacuated from Vietnam. These were South Vietnamese considered at "high risk" from the North Vietnamese who were on the very doorstep of Saigon. Now there were just eleven Marines on the roof of the Embassy, waiting for a helicopter to take them to the American aircraft carriers and destroyers off the coast of Vietnam in the South China Sea. Throughout the previous day 1,500 Americans and 5,600 Vietnamese had been flown to the evacuation fleet, from Saigon and from Tan Son Nhut airbase to the north of the city.

As the Marines waited, crouched down on the roof of the Embassy for fear of being shot at by disenchanted South Vietnamese soldiers, other Vietnamese tried to force a way onto the roof in a last desperate bid to be evacuated. Many who had thought they were to be taken out of Vietnam had, in the final confusion, been left behind. The door to the roof area was barricaded with lockers and air-conditioning units; through the window in the door enquiring arms sought to find a way in. One of the Marines was given the job of fighting them off, forcing the arms into the broken glass.

After two hours a Chinook 46 helicopter, escorted by helicopter gunships, appeared from the south east to take the last American soldiers out of Vietnam. To make their escape they hurled tear gas grenades into the crowds of Vietnamese inside the Embassy compound. The helicopter blades sucked the choking gas inside the cabin, for the moment blinding the pilots and their Marine passengers.

It was 7.53 a.m. when the last American left Vietnam and America's fifteen-year involvement in the country ended. At 11 a.m. the Presidential Palace in Saigon was symbolically occupied by the North Vietnamese. By noon, North Vietnamese flags flew from every building. Saigon was renamed Ho Chi Minh City.

The North Vietnamese advance on Saigon

The final offensive by the North Vietnamese against the South, which after thirty years of fighting would unify Vietnam again, began in December 1974. The province of Phuoc Long, close to Saigon, was chosen for an attack by the North, to test South Vietnamese, and American, resolve. The provincial capital, Phuoc Binh, was taken on 7th January, 1975. The Phuoc Long offensive was a taste of what was to come.

Vietnam before re-unification in 1973.

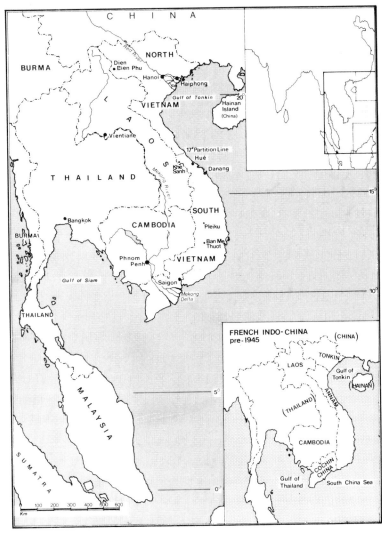

General Van Tien Dung (pronounced "Zung"), Commander of the North Vietnamese forces, was convinced that the US had no further taste to fight in Vietnam. The Tet Offensive of 1968 had destroyed the will both of the US forces in Vietnam and of the American people to persevere with a war that was daily looking more unwinnable. Popular protest against the US war in Vietnam had grown throughout the world. General Dung was sure, too, that there would be no further B52 bombing raids against Hanoi and the North, for the US had turned in on itself following the disgrace of President Richard Nixon in the Watergate scandal of 1973. After the Paris Peace Agreement of 1973 most American forces had left Vietnam and American aid to President Thieu of South Vietnam had gradually declined. Several thousand American soldiers remained, to aid the "Vietnamization" of the war, but South Vietnamese troops (ARVN) were now responsible for the security of the South. Finally General Dung was confident that, although the United States was a superpower, "a small country, with a small land mass and small population which knows how to consolidate and knows its leadership could defeat a greater power."

The fall of Phuoc Long in January 1975 illustrated the inability of the ARVN to hold back a North Vietnamese advance. When there was no American reaction, except to accuse the North Vietnamese government in Hanoi of breaking the Paris Peace Agreement, the North Vietnamese leadership recognized that "the moment had come to undertake the last battle to liberate the South". This was to take just four months, much to the surprise of the North Vietnamese who had been prepared for a two-year struggle.

Ban Me Thuot, 10th March, 1975

Given the successes of the North Vietnamese General Dung decided to increase his forces in the South. The "Ho Chi Minh trail" from the North to the South had been strengthened with a fuel pipe line now along most of its route. New troops, military materials and supplies travelled this way. In February 1975 Dung, disguised as a Vietnamese peasant, had travelled to the South with Le Duc Tho, the most important political figure in the North. To hide the fact that Dung was no longer in Hanoi, a double travelled in his car every morning to army headquarters and messages were transmitted in his name.

Dung's presence in the South was not known to the US

Central Intelligence Agency (CIA) or to the South Vietnamese, nor was the presence of his troops, thousands of whom were concentrated in the Western Highlands. Moving in radio silence, three divisions of North Vietnamese troops assembled in the area around Ban Me Thuot, capture of which would give complete control of the Highlands.

The day before the attack General Dung called his officers together. "I told them, there are two lines from a poem which burn in my heart, 'For thirty years our land has taken up the gun, yet still the disc of our moon is split in two'." The troops waited, their tanks hidden in villages twenty miles from Ban Me Thuot. The palm trees in which they were hidden were sawn three-quarters through so that at a moment's notice they could race forward to their target. Then, as they waited, a herd of elephants charged them. Had they fired at them they would have betrayed their position. Dung did not hesitate to order a retreat. "There's nothing wrong with running from elephants."

The surprise elephant attack did not delay Dung's assault on Ban Me Thuot. On 10th March rockets and artillery poured into the ARVN 23rd Division headquarters there. The South Vietnamese troops were taken entirely by surprise. With no reinforcements and little defence from the air they had no alternative but to surrender. The battle for Ban Me Thuot was over in thirty hours. North Vietnamese forces could now sweep to the central coast and then head south to Saigon. CIA analysts in Saigon foresaw that, without a massive deployment of US ground forces, a North Vietnamese victory was inevitable. But no such use of American forces was possible by now, for US aid to South Vietnam was not only being cut back; within three months it would be cut off completely.

President Thieu decided to withdraw his troops from the Highlands and their position to the north, and to fall back to the southern delta which was the most important economic zone in the country. Thieu considered the withdrawal to be his only option. It was little short of a disaster.

A rumour spread that Thieu had offered the North Vietnamese half of South Vietnam. Civilians fled, with withdrawing troops, to the coast. Highway 7 was chosen for the withdrawal, a narrow, winding road which was soon attacked by the North Vietnamese. In the ensuing panic soldiers fled, crushing civilians under the wheels and tracks of their vehicles. Only one in four ever reached the coast for evacuation by sea.

Hué, 21st-25th March

North Vietnamese troops in battle on the outskirts of Hué.

Dung now moved to two important cities, Hué, the ancient capital of Vietnam, and Da Nang, the second city of the South and the main port for the evacuation of Thieu's army. "Hundreds of thousands of vehicles ran bumper to bumper day and night" in Dung's advance, acting on his slogan "Lightning speed, daring and more daring".

On 21st March Dung's troops moved to encircle Hué. For three days their artillery, Soviet 130mm guns, bombarded the outer edge of the city. ARVN troops abandoned Hué and on 25th March the North Vietnamese were able to hoist their flag over the main gate. When Dung heard of the fall of Hué he treated himself to a cigarette, a pleasure he reserved for himself "whenever I solve some thorny problem, or receive some news of outstanding conquests".

Da Nang, 30th March, 1975

Fighting to get on board a helicopter frequently occurred in the evacuation of South Vietnamese towns as the troops from the North closed on Saigon. Here, at Nha Trang, an American official punches a man to keep him from boarding an already over-loaded helicopter.

At Da Nang, Dung's next target, refugees had swelled the population to three million. Escape was impossible. Many drowned attempting to get away in the few boats that were available. An American airlift was cancelled when soldiers and civilians fought for seats. The ARVN commander of Da Nang deserted his troops, to be followed by most of his officers. Soldiers took off their uniforms and disguised themselves as civilians. Da Nang surrendered on 30th March, just thirty-two hours after being surrounded by troops from the North.

And on to Saigon

The advance of the North Vietnamese was now unstoppable, and they had decided to go for total victory. Ho Chi Minh's birthday would be celebrated in Saigon on 19th May; therefore the city would have to be taken by 1st May. Dung's army was literally racing towards Saigon. Only at Xuan Loc, a small provincial capital thirty-eight miles to the north east, was there any spirited resistance. Dung described the battle as "fierce and cruel from the very first days". Five thousand ARVN held back the numerically stronger North Vietnamese who were forced to attack and counter-attack. "Our division had to organize many assaults, striking and striking again to destroy each target and had to repel many enemy counter-attacks." Xuan Loc held out against the North Vietnamese from 9th to 21st April.

There was nothing to hold back the advance of Dung's troops on Saigon. As Xuan Loc fell, President Thieu resigned. As he sped to the airport to be whisked away into exile with (it was reported) between two and three tons of gold, the North Vietnamese closed in on the city. On the streets the people of Saigon went about their everyday business; many still felt that "something would happen" so that they would control a part of Vietnam. They were living in a fantasy world. Within a week Saigon was to fall and Vietnam was to become one country again.

At the headquarters of the "Ho Chi Minh" campaign for the final assault on Saigon in late April 1975. Seated are General Van Tien Dung (left), Le Duc Tho (centre) and Pham Hang who was in charge of the Saigon area during the campaign.

How the Americans had decided on "peace"

By the end of the 1960s in the United States support for the Vietnam war had waned. Each month a thousand bodies were flown home from Vietnam bringing sorrow to every town and city. Daily the war could be seen on television, its full horror brought into the living room of every American family. "Peace Now" became not only the slogan at demonstrations but the topic of conversation in millions of Americans' houses. In October 1967 a mass demonstration of 50,000 people at the Lincoln Memorial in Washington D.C. heard Dr Benjamin Spock, amongst others, declare: "The enemy, we believe, is Lyndon B. Johnson [the US President]". The demonstration ended with over a thousand people arrested after fighting in the streets and attempts to invade the Pentagon, the US military nerve centre. The Washington demonstration was the culmination of popular protest against the war, which had built up in the US in the last half of the decade.

In March 1968 President Johnson made an important television speech. He began: "Tonight, I want to speak to you about peace in Vietnam, and South East Asia. No other question so preoccupies our people." He announced that the level of troops in Vietnam had been frozen, that the air war against the North would be limited, and that a negotiated end to the war would be sought with North Vietnam's leaders. The Paris Peace negotiations between Americans and North Vietnamese began in May 1968.

How the American resolve had been broken

More than any other event of the Vietnam war, the Tet Offensive at the beginning of 1968 had served to break the resolve not just of the US Military but also of American society in general to continue with the war. At the end of 1967 US Military confidence had been high; a "light at the end of the tunnel" could be discerned. The light was an illusion, for from July 1967 General Giap, North Vietnam's most experienced military leader, was preparing a general attack on Vietnamese cities in order to undermine the morale of the American forces and destroy South Vietnamese confidence in American protection.

The attack began on 31st January, 1968, the lunar New Year, or "Tet" as it is known to the Vietnamese. The first target was the* American Embassy in Saigon itself. Six hundred Viet Cong (the name given to members of the National Liberation Front – NLF – operating in the South) had entered Saigon, hidden in trucks or wheeling bicycles and disguised as people from the countryside. At the Embassy gates US Marines quickly killed the first group of attackers but, while this was going on, other Viet Cong had blown a hole in the wall to the grounds. A fierce and bloody battle began against Marines and diplomats. This was filmed at close hand and televised around the world. It may have been a small incident – all the Viet Cong attackers of the US Embassy were killed within six hours – but its psychological effect was important, boosting the morale of the North, undermining that of the Americans and South Vietnamese.

As Saigon was under siege by the Viet Cong, so, too, were a hundred other towns and cities. The Viet Cong in Saigon, whose numbers had increased to 4,000, fought street battles for days, with attacks on the Presidential Palace and the South Vietnamese Military Headquarters. Bomb and rocket attacks against the Viet Cong set parts of Saigon alight, leaving civilians homeless and at risk from the firing from both sides. Throughout South Vietnam thousands of Vietnamese were arrested as Viet Cong suspects.

Outside Hué, the ancient capital of Vietnam with its special cultural and religious importance, North Vietnamese regular troops threw off their disguises to reveal their army uniforms. Within a day they had successfully taken most of the city and the North Vietnamese flag flew over the citadel. Whilst the Tet Offensive was largely defeated within two weeks, Hué remained as an example of North Vietnamese control. Vast quantities of US military hardware and troops were airlifted to the areas around the city. The battle for Hué was one of the bloodiest of the war. This was not warfare from a distance, as so much of the war had been for the Americans, but conventional hand-to-hand, door-to-door fighting. The North Vietnamese struggled tenaciously to hold Hué, fighting back the assaults by US Marines. After a month the North Vietnamese were forced back to the citadel, a fortress which had once been the Imperial Palace of Vietnam. There they were shelled at point-blank range and bombed from the air. Hué was completely devastated, its wooden houses destroyed, its historic buildings reduced to rubble. The city had been destroyed in order to "save" it.

US Marines were unused to the fierce, hand-to-hand fighting which occurred during the battle for Hué in 1968. Their capture of Hué on 25th February signalled the end of the Tet Offensive.

Hué fell to the superior fire power of the US Marines on 25th February, 1968. The Tet Offensive was over. Both sides claimed victory. The North Vietnamese saw it as a strategic victory; the US as an outright success. The cost in lives was horrendous. In Hué alone, 5,800 civilians died, along with 400 South Vietnamese troops (ARVN) and 142 US Marines. General Westmoreland, who led US troops in Vietnam, described the offensive as "the turning point of the war. It could have been a turning point for victory, but it was the turning point of failure."

Also in early 1968 the seventy-seven-day siege of Khe Sanh led to the questioning of America's role in Vietnam. The North Vietnamese attack on the US base began at dawn on 21st January. On that day alone 300 artillery rounds landed with pin-point accuracy on the base, killing 18 Marines and destroying a munitions dump containing 1,500 tons of explosives. The Americans were a visible, concentrated target at Khe Sanh, on a plateau half a mile long and a quarter of a mile wide. By the end of the day they were completely encircled by crack North Vietnamese troops. The 3,500 Marines were outnumbered by at least four to one. General Giap had planned this attack too.

The US President, Lyndon Johnson, saw the siege as a test of America's military might and resolve. He demanded a written commitment from the Military – "signed in blood" – that Khe Sanh would not fall to the Vietnamese. "The eyes of the nation, the eyes of the entire world, are on that little brave band of defenders who hold the pass at Khe Sanh." With the prompting of the President, his Commander-in-Chief, General Westmoreland decided to hold Khe Sanh, saying that this was to prevent the North Vietnamese from moving closer to encircle Saigon. Yet before the North Vietnamese attack, Khe Sanh had not been seen as an important base blocking the North Vietnamese advance.

American and North Vietnamese artillery exchanged shells, the US returning twenty for every one they received. Even so, there was no let-up in the attack by the North Vietnamese nor in the advance of their infantry who could be heard at night digging their trenches closer to the base. US air attacks – 300 a day, one bombing raid every five minutes – did not deter the Vietnamese advance. Electronic sensors dropped around Khe Sanh gave accurate positions of North Vietnamese targets against which "Operation Niagara", a veritable waterfall of bombs, was launched. Huge B52 bombers dropped the equivalent in destructive power of five Hiroshima-sized bombs in the Khe Sanh area. Every day 5,000 bombs were dropped, the highest concentration in the history of warfare. A two-mile area around Khe Sanh was reduced to rubble. Still the North Vietnamese advanced.

Supplies were parachuted into the base or pushed out of slow-moving planes. Only the wounded were evacuated. Many Marines hoped for wounds so as to escape the daily pounding from the encircling Vietnamese, and from the

The battle for Khe Sanh was brought daily into the homes of Americans by television reports. Pictures of the fighting, the injuries suffered and the loss of life added greatly to American disenchantment with the war in Vietnam. President Johnson was also said to have been greatly influenced by television coverage of the war. During Tet and Khe Sanh he had three huge televisions, tuned to the three major networks, and would study them as a source of information before he received official reports from the field.

The growth of an anti-war movement throughout the United States in the 1960s was an important factor in the country's disillusionment with the Vietnam war.

misery of living in trenches which they shared with the local rat population.

The "Khe Sanh Story" became headline news in the American press, and filled television news time, fuelling America's growing disenchantment with the war. This was a war that America was supposed to be winning and yet here were America's youth daily being killed and maimed, defending a base 9,000 miles away, and with no end in sight to their suffering. The continuation of the war clearly helped the North Vietnamese cause.

In mid-March the North Vietnamese began to leave Khe Sanh, their withdrawal attacked from the air. The base could now be relieved and on 6th April relief forces moved in. The

15

A memorial service for American soldiers in South Vietnam, 1968.

siege had left 1,600 North Vietnamese dead, 205 Marines killed and a further 800 badly wounded. Khe Sanh was later abandoned by the United States, bringing into question its costly defence. In the US one in five Americans was now against the war. The Paris Peace negotiations were about to begin.

Official and unofficial peace talks

The Paris Peace talks began in May 1968 but little progress was made. The first seven months of deliberations resolved only the size and shape of the table to be used for the negotiations and where the respective negotiators would sit around it. The North Vietnamese were not prepared to discuss anything with the representatives from Saigon since to do so would imply that they recognized them as a legitimate government.

In the meantime there was a change of American president. When he had announced the peace talks, President Johnson had also announced that he would not seek nor accept the nomination of the Democratic Party for the coming presidential election. Withdrawing from the election battle, to concentrate on Vietnam, he left the field to other candidates in his party who took an anti-war position, such as Robert Kennedy and Hubert Humphrey. Had the Democrats won the presidential election, a rapid peace solution might well have been sought. But it was not to be. On 5th November, 1968, it was the Republican Richard Nixon who was elected President of the United States, by a narrow margin. In his election campaign he had emphasized "de-Americanization" of the war.

"The greatest honour that history can bestow is the title of peacemaker," President Nixon said in his inaugural speech. As far as Vietnam was concerned, he had offered nothing more than "de-Americanization" and "Peace with honour". One of President Johnson's last acts as President had been to halt the aerial and naval bombardment of North Vietnam. Nixon was prepared to re-invigorate, even escalate, the war.

Even before he was elected President, Nixon had told one of his assistants that he wanted the North Vietnamese to believe that he had reached the point where he might do *anything* to stop their advance. He spoke of his "Madman Theory". He wanted the North Vietnamese to know that, because of his obsessional hatred of communism, he could not be restrained in his efforts to combat its spreading and would even be prepared to use nuclear weapons to this end. Vietnam, according to Nixon, was to be a mere "sideshow" where America's position in relation to the other superpowers, China and the Soviet Union, could be acted out. Nixon hoped to play off China and the Soviet Union against one another and in the process to exact concessions from either side. For this the United States needed to continue to appear a strong force in Vietnam. The war had to be pursued.

Now President, Richard Nixon and his Secretary of State Henry Kissinger began a secret war against Vietnam's neighbour, Cambodia (today called Kampuchea). This only became known about in 1973. "Operation Menu" (consisting of Operations Breakfast, Lunch, Snack, Dinner, Dessert and Supper) was the high-level bombing of the Fish Hook and Parrot's Beak, the small curve of Cambodia to the north west of Saigon, where the North Vietnamese regional headquarters (COSVN) were thought to be. The bombardment which began on 18th March, 1969, increased to every part of Cambodia where the North Vietnamese were *believed* to be, even if this included civilian areas. In the next fourteen months, the United States dropped on Cambodia four times the tonnage of bombs that had fallen on Japan during the Second World War. In all, there were 3,650 B52 raids on the country whose only crime was to lie adjacent to Vietnam. In President Nixon's view, "It was enemy territory – it was not Cambodian territory, and we had every right, legally and morally to take what action was necessary to protect our forces." The bombing brought neither response nor concession from the North Vietnamese.

★   ★   ★   ★   ★   ★   ★

At the Paris Peace talks (expanded to include the NLF as well as North Vietnam and the USA), the North Vietnamese demands were for an American Military withdrawal to allow North and South Vietnam to agree upon a political solution. Henry Kissinger proposed the withdrawal of US and North Vietnamese troops over a period of a year, the release of prisoners, a supervised cease-fire and elections. The Vietnamese played for time, regrouping and strengthening their forces.

In July 1969 Richard Nixon sent a private letter to Ho Chi Minh, leader of the Viet Minh, in Hanoi. He suggested that secret talks be held between Henry Kissinger, his Secretary of State, and Le Duc Tho, North Vietnam's most experienced negotiator. Ho Chi Minh agreed and the first secret meeting took place in August 1969 in Paris. Over the next two and a half years Kissinger made fifteen trips to Paris in utmost secrecy. Using the presidential plane, he and his assistants

In June 1969 President Nixon met South Vietnam's President, Nguyen Van Thieu, on Midway Island in the Pacific. President Nixon announced that he was withdrawing 25,000 men from Vietnam as an encouragement to peace talks, and as a show of confidence in South Vietnam's army. "Vietnamization" had begun.

would leave Washington on Saturdays and fly to central France where they would transfer to a private jet arranged by the French President, Georges Pompidou. Then they would go to an apartment in Paris to rest, before discussion with Le Duc Tho all day Sunday. Because of the time difference between Washington and Paris, it was possible for Kissinger to be in his office on Monday morning as if he had never been out of the United States.

At the secret meetings Kissinger played on President Nixon's "Madman Theory". Henry Kissinger was the "good guy", Nixon the "bad guy". He would say: "Look. I represent this crazy fellow Nixon, and there's no telling what he might do. I am a very reasonable man. I am a man of peace. But there's no telling what Nixon might do. So you'd better deal with me because I am going to be much easier to get along with than he is." Whenever there were obstacles to agreement, Nixon would initiate a bombing or attack so that Kissinger could return to the negotiating table to say: "See what happens when you don't make your deal with me – he back there in the White House does something crazy!" Le Duc Tho was not pressured by Kissinger into making any hurried decision. While the discussions continued North Vietnam was rebuilding, preparing for the final victory against the South. Not even the bombing of Cambodia drew concessions from Le Duc Tho who, throughout the discussions, smiled at Kissinger, never saying yes nor ever saying no. Behind this facade he was often angry. "Rage grips me," he said to his assistants. "So many years their heels have crushed our country, a thousand, thousand oppressions."

★ ★ ★ ★ ★ ★ ★

By the 1970s President Nixon had to contend with the flagging morale of US troops in Vietnam as well as with growing discontent with the war at home. Increasingly, young men were looking for ways to avoid their draft into the Military. Anti-war demonstrations had become more violent. They were often led by wounded veterans returned from Vietnam who publicly burned their uniforms and medal ribbons. In 1970, at Kent State University in Ohio, National Guardsmen opened fire on students protesting about US actions in Vietnam. Four were killed, eleven wounded. A wave of revulsion travelled across America.

A secret study of US policies and actions in Vietnam from 1945 to 1968 had been commissioned by the US Defense Department. This study, known as the *Pentagon Papers*, was leaked to the press, revealing American atrocities like that at My Lai. At this village in 1968 Lieutenant William Calley had thrown grenades into Vietnamese peasants' homes, and mown down women and children with automatic weapons. Other men, women and children were rounded up and killed. Seven hundred people had been murdered. My Lai was one example of the brutalizing way in which the war was conducted. Such revelations added to the discontent in the US.

★ ★ ★ ★ ★ ★ ★

In 1972, to win political support as a "peacemaker", President Nixon revealed that the secret talks between Kissinger and Le Duc Tho had been going on. He announced that an agreement would be signed under which all US forces would be withdrawn and a cease-fire observed. Also as part of the terms, supervised elections would be held within six months of signing the agreement. President Thieu in Saigon would step down before seeking re-election. These terms were no different from those proposed in 1969 in earlier talks.

On 30th March, 1972, 120,000 North Vietnamese troops moved across the 17th Parallel, the line dividing the North from the South. With tanks and armoured vehicles they swept into three provinces. It is not clear whether they were attempting to increase their numbers of troops inside the South before the cease-fire, or whether they had discounted further US opposition. What is clear is that they had not imagined the awesome response of President Nixon. He immediately ordered massive attacks from the air in support of ARVN forces and the bombardment of areas close to Hanoi and Haiphong. The ports of Hanoi and Haiphong were mined, so as to keep out supplies from the Soviet Union.

The North Vietnamese were unable to continue their fight against the American air attacks and, in October, returned to the Paris Peace talks where a military settlement was proposed. A cease-fire, leaving the North Vietnamese where they were in the South, was agreed, in return for the complete withdrawal of US troops and an exchange of prisoners. Perhaps it was clear to the North Vietnamese that Richard Nixon was about to be re-elected for a second term of office and that they would have to continue to negotiate with him. The settlement would leave 150,000 North Vietnamese in place in South Vietnam and, although it gave the US the "honourable" peace that President Nixon had spoken of in 1968, all the bombing of the intervening years had been for nothing. The only stumbling block to the signing of the settlement was to obtain the agreement of President Thieu of South Vietnam.

★   ★   ★   ★   ★   ★   ★

Despite the closeness of an agreement the "Madman Theory" had life still left in it. President Thieu was sceptical of a number of points in the settlement and finally rejected the terms outright. When Nixon asked the North Vietnamese for a delay, their response was to broadcast the full terms of the agreement and the date, 31st October, 1972, that had been set for its signing. Kissinger could not sign without President Thieu's agreement and when this was not forthcoming he began secretly meeting Le Duc Tho again in Paris, to present some sixty proposed changes that had come from President Thieu. Kissinger warned Le Duc Tho, on President Nixon's orders, that if the talks broke down the US would again resort to a huge demonstration of military might. Kissinger's own opinion was that the war would only be ended with a brutal show of force to damage the North Vietnamese and bring them back to the negotiating table.

When the Christmas bombing of Hanoi and Haiphong began, it brought condemnation from all over the world. The

The US war against Vietnam brought condemnation from round the world as these Cuban stamps of 1966 show. The Christmas bombing of Hanoi and Haiphong was especially condemned.

horrific raids were described as "grotesque", "genocide" and "a crime against humanity". The *Times* wrote: "This is not the conduct of a man who wants peace very badly." On the first day of the raids, 18th December, 121 B52s rained down bombs on the two cities. Three of the planes, costing $8 million each, were destroyed by surface-to-air missiles (SAMs). The North Vietnamese defenders were at their battle stations twenty-four hours each day, but the ferocity of the US attack was unparalleled in the history of warfare. On the third day of the raid the North Vietnamese, through careful study of the B52s' flight paths, were able to down a further six of the enormous bombers. Captured American pilots told journalists of their surprise not to see any military targets in the areas they had bombed.

After a pause for Christmas day the bombing recommenced with greater ferocity. By 29th December 100,000 bombs had fallen on Hanoi and Haiphong, the equivalent in destructive force of five of the atomic bombs dropped on Hiroshima. One can only guess at the numbers of civilian deaths that resulted.

Negotiations began again in Paris and the Paris Peace Agreement was finally signed on 23rd January, 1973. A cease-fire was to take effect four days later.

    ★   ★   ★   ★   ★   ★   ★   ★

Under the Paris Peace Agreement most US forces left Vietnam. A force of several thousand remained to aid the "Vietnamization" of the war, but South Vietnamese troops (ARVN) were now to be responsible for the security of the South.

Henry Kissinger, America's chief negotiator and special adviser to President Nixon, sits on the right (centre) at the Paris Peace Talks, facing Le Duc Tho, North Vietnam's main negotiator. The Peace Agreement of 1973 was days away.

Fighting did not stop; an average of one thousand ARVN died each month between 1973 and 1975 in continuous battles to secure control of the countryside. President Thieu was sure that Washington expected the collapse of the South six months after the Peace signing. American military and economic aid declined and by late 1974, when General Dung was beginning his final offensive and preparing to take Saigon, Thieu claimed that he was without helicopter and artillery replacements and that his US air support was non-existent. Graham Martin, US Ambassador in Saigon, pleaded in vain with his government for aid for the South. The fall of Saigon to the North Vietnamese looked inevitable.

"Vietnamization". The airbase at Long Binh, the largest built by the Americans in Vietnam, is handed over to South Vietnamese forces.

The last day in Saigon:
30th April, 1975

On 23rd April, 1975, American CIA officials in Saigon learned that the North Vietnamese Army was to attack the city from five directions and to occupy it within a week. General Dung had more than 100,000 troops poised ready to take Saigon and was prepared to use whatever force was necessary. Yet he preferred the minimum of bloodshed; enough blood had already been lost in Vietnam – 57,000 American soldiers killed and 2 million North Vietnamese – and, for that reason, the Americans in Saigon were given a little more time in which to evacuate their own people and their South Vietnamese allies.

Throughout April, at an accelerating rate as the North Vietnamese advanced towards Saigon, nearly 50,000 South Vietnamese had been flown out of the city from Tan Son Nhut airbase, just to the north, in huge C-130 planes. Americans continued to work at their desks, since it was feared that their evacuation would create a complete panic in Saigon. That was soon to come, however.

On 29th April pilots of the C-130s at Tan Son Nhut saw what they thought was a thunderstorm getting closer. As the "storm" changed colour they realized they were watching rockets and mortars from the North Vietnamese, which rained down upon them with great accuracy. A fuel truck and the control tower were hit in the first minute of the attack. A rocket exploded under the wing of one of the C-130s. US Marines guarding the base were killed outright.

In Saigon, Frank Snepp, who worked for the CIA, rolled out of bed, groping around on the floor for his helmet and flak jacket. Looking out of the window of his apartment he could see huge fire balls rising into the night sky. The horizon pulsed with artillery flashes.

The runways had been damaged and covered in debris from the attack. It was doubtful if the airport could be used again. Yet US Ambassador Graham Martin, against the advice of his staff, decided to make a tour of inspection himself. He was optimistic that the runways could be opened to speed up the evacuation of all those Vietnamese to whom, he felt, the Americans had a moral obligation. Many Vietnamese had worked with, and for, the Americans and would be at risk from the North Vietnamese who were poised to take Saigon and unify the country again.

Ambassador Martin was advised that no more C-130s could land in the chaos of debris covering the airport runways and so those planes on their way to Saigon were ordered to return to base at Honolulu. The attack on the airbase by the North Vietnamese had been a signal of their growing impatience at the Americans' slowness over the evacuation and of their concern that the Americans were attempting to thwart their final victory or even seeking justification for a last-minute intervention. There was now only one option open to Ambassador Martin: Option IV, a total evacuation by helicopter.

The American Service Radio in Saigon played "I'm dreaming of a White Christmas" and gave a false weather report: "It is 105 degrees and rising" – the pre-arranged signal for the final evacuation. American officials, businessmen, journalists and their close Vietnamese helpers and friends dropped whatever they were doing to race to the US Embassy or one of the twelve other helicopter roof-top landing areas. Huge crowds of Vietnamese blocked the gates of the Embassy, fighting to get in. Marines found great difficulty in deciding who should be allowed in and who kept out.

Panic and confusion characterized the American withdrawal. Inside the Embassy grounds the incinerators worked non-stop, destroying incriminating intelligence documents. Two large canvas bags containing US $2 million, the Ambassador's special contingency fund, were dragged to the furnaces; they were to be burned also. Just as they were hurled inside, the Ambassador changed his mind. He wanted to hang on to the money a little longer. Some of it was saved, only later to be scattered through Saigon by the downdraft of a descending helicopter. Over $80,000 were taken by an American official who gave the money to his Vietnamese girlfriend who was able to smuggle it out of the country inside her dress.

US Marines were brought into Vietnam again, for the first time since the evacuation of US troops after the Paris Peace Agreement of 1973. This time they were to oversee the evacuation and provide security. Helicopters were now flying in and out of Saigon, using the Embassy courtyard and roof as landing-pads, to ferry people to the US fleet in the South China Sea. Those needing to go seemed to make up a never-ending stream of people. As well as Vietnamese officials and military personnel went secretaries, friends and servants to the Americans. While Americans and Vietnamese crammed aboard huge helicopters, and thousands more fought for the chance, barges in Saigon harbour, sent to assist in the evacuation, were largely ignored. Their existence was kept secret, even from the staff of the US Embassy, for fear of causing a stampede. Had the barges been more efficiently used, the hundreds of "high-risk" Vietnamese left behind might well have been evacuated along with the rest. Frank Snepp was later to say: "We abandoned so many we should have rescued."

Vietnamese were not the only ones having trouble getting out. American and other foreign journalists had to fight their way in to the US Embassy. Keyes Beech of the *Chicago Daily News* described his experience:

"Once we moved into that seething mass we ceased to be correspondents. We were only men fighting for our lives, scratching, clawing, pushing ever closer to that wall. We were like animals.

There were a pair of Marines on the wall. They were trying to help us and kicked the Vietnamese down. One of them looked down at me. "Help me" I pleaded. "Please help me." That Marine helped me. He reached down with his long, muscular arm and pulled me up as if I were a helpless child."

His Vietnamese and Japanese friends were left outside the Embassy gates. The Marines could not, or would not, pull them over the wall.

The evacuation became a free-for-all, with American officials putting their friends to the top of the waiting list; others pulled in friends and colleagues from the vast crowds besieging the Embassy gates. The number of people within the grounds of the Embassy grew. When members of Saigon's police force were pulled over the high wall by Marines, it proved too much for the waiting crowd. Scores fought to get over. Marines fought them back, clubbing them with rifles, prising off fingers and hands which were clinging to the wall.

As the evacuation neared completion General Dung and his officers prepared for the final assault on Saigon.

"After a one-day offensive on all fronts we realized that the situation had developed very favourably as we had anticipated. By midnight 29th April the whole of our striking force was fully prepared for the push into Saigon. The air was tense, as though at the raising of a magic hatchet". (Dung)

Helicopters were pushed into the South China Sea, from US aircraft carriers, so as to make room for others to land in the final hours of the evacuation of Saigon.

The Americans had taken long enough with their evacuation. The time was now right for the army to attack.

There were few Americans left at the Embassy. Ambassador Martin was one of the last, finally ordered to leave by President Ford. There was no chance to pack; the treasured possessions of a lifetime had to be left behind. As his helicopter lifted above Saigon, Graham Martin could see Tan Son Nhut airbase in flames. Twenty minutes later, as the helicopter crossed the coast and the sun was beginning to rise, scores of boats of all shapes and sizes could be seen below, sailing out to the evacuation fleet. They would later be joined by South Vietnamese helicopter pilots who ditched their US planes in the sea alongside the US fleet, in their desperation to escape. From the US aircraft carriers dozens of helicopters, each worth $250,000, were pushed into the sea to make room for others to land. On that last day 7,000 Vietnamese and Americans were taken out of Saigon.

Ambassador Martin described his mood as "one of enormous relief". The final hours of the war were bloodless.

★　★　★　★　★　★　★

General Dung telephoned his superiors in Hanoi, and then sent a radio message to his battery Commanders in the east of Saigon, ordering them to stop the bombardment of Tan Son Nhut airbase so that their army could advance on the city. Dung directed his Commanders to make "deep thrusts, to advance to predetermined points" into Saigon. His command post on the outskirts of the city was buzzing with activity. He described how "flashlights, hurricane lamps and searchlights lit the alleys leading to it. Electric lights lit up the war room. Grey-haired and black-haired officers carefully studied a map, tracing red arrows which pointed at the pre-selected major objectives in Saigon. Behind the war room, a row of telephone sets worked incessantly." (*Our Great Spring Victory*, Van Tien Dung, 1977)

When they received the news that the North Vietnamese troops had liberated Saigon, Dung and the other army leaders jumped up and down with joy. They embraced one another. Some even carried their comrades round on their shoulders. "The sound of applause, laughter, and happy, noisy chattering," Dung wrote, "was as festive as if spring had just burst upon us. It was an indescribably joyous scene."

In Hanoi, on hearing the news, the people poured out onto the streets, lighting fire-crackers, throwing flowers and waving flags, singing, laughing, enjoying this very special day. After thirty years of war the people celebrated the peace that had finally come and with it the uniting of their country. Many thought of Ho Chi Minh who had not lived long enough to enjoy the victory but whose inspiration and example had made the victory possible. Ho had died on 3rd September, 1969, aged 79. He had founded the Democratic Republic of Vietnam and been its leader for nearly a quarter of a century.

★　★　★　★　★　★　★

In the time between the flight of the last Americans and the entry of General Dung's forces into Saigon, the poor of the city looted many buildings. High on the list were the Embassies, now empty, their occupants taken out in the airlift. Everything was stripped from them; even the chandeliers were carried away.

★   ★   ★   ★   ★   ★   ★

A North Vietnamese tank enters the grounds of the Presidential Palace in Saigon. Soon Saigon is to be no more and is renamed Ho Chi Minh City.

The North Vietnamese troops and the NLF entered Saigon in style. A tank rammed the ornate metal gates of the Presidential Palace and, although pieces of metal were broken off, the gates refused to open. Once the gates were unlocked, the first tank raced into the Palace grounds, firing a salute as it entered. Then, for the benefit of the few journalists still in Saigon, the symbolic taking of the Presidential Palace was performed by the tanks all over again.

Their salutes, fired in the air, terrified the soldiers who had acted as guards at the Palace.

A soldier with the NLF flag held high above his head then ran into the Palace to appear a little later on one of the terraces, waving the flag round and round above him. Next he appeared on the roof where he took down the red and yellow stripes of the Saigon regime and hoisted the NLF flag.

More tanks, lorries and troops poured into Saigon's streets. All the vehicles and the helmets of the troops were covered in camouflaging leaves. The troops assembled in one of the broad avenues leading up to the Palace. Dressed in green uniforms, with red armbands and flashes on their rifles, they appeared relaxed and confident in this unfamiliar city. The South Vietnamese army, thick on the ground only hours before, had disappeared as if by magic. The only evidence that they had ever existed in Saigon was piles of clothes, boots and guns at the side of the road. Young men in their underpants, attempting to look nonchalant, hung around in doorways as if the war had had nothing to do with them. Groups of captured South Vietnamese soldiers were made to remove their uniforms and sit in the shade.

The North Vietnamese soldiers were the source of great interest to the people of Saigon who plied them with questions after having plucked up the courage to leave their homes. How would they be treated? The North Vietnamese replied gently and reassuringly. No, there would be no ill-treatment. No, nobody would be forced to marry anyone else. No, there would be no bloodbath. The war was over. And, Yes, we do eat rice just like you. Most of the troops came from the North. A few guerrillas of the Viet Cong, from the South itself, carrying antiquated weapons, with strange-shaped bombs strapped to their waists, and some of them barefooted, explored Saigon in twos and threes. The next day the Navy arrived in the harbour and the Air Force flew into Tan Son Nhut. The war was over for all of them. This was a time for sight-seeing.

THE INVESTIGATION

How did the United States become involved in Vietnam? – 1 To 1954: Supporting the French

The French in Vietnam

Before the Americans became involved in Vietnam it was occupied by the French. By 1867 France was in control of Cochin China, the name given at that time to the southern part of the country, and this was turned into a French colony. By 1884 the French had gone on to take the remaining areas of Annam and Tonkin. (See the inset map on page 5.) Armed opposition to French control of these areas lasted until 1917, by which time the French had imposed their harsh authority upon the whole of Vietnam. By 1930 there were more French civil servants in Vietnam than British ones in India whose population was more than twelve times as large. Cochin China was the most profitable area of Vietnam for the French, although profits went only to a small group of investors.

A nationalist movement developed in Vietnam made up of educated Vietnamese with support from the ranks of the 100,000 Vietnamese soldiers who had fought alongside the French against Germany in the First World War. The French resisted any suggestion of reforms, and were against the idea of independence for Vietnam. Those involved in the nationalist movement were jailed and harshly treated. A nationalist rebellion in 1930 was quickly suppressed.

Japanese occupation of Indo-China

The occupation of Indo-China by the Japanese during the Second World War gave further momentum to the growing nationalist movement. The French administration in Vietnam was willing to collaborate with the Japanese and so control of Vietnam remained in French hands.

Ho Chi Minh and the Viet Minh

Opposition to the Japanese occupation was led by the Indo-Chinese Communist Party. In May 1941 what was left of this

Party, after a serious military defeat by the French, met Ho Chi Minh, already known as a major communist and Vietnamese nationalist, in Southern China, close to the border with Tonkin. Here the Viet Nam Doc Lap Dong Minh Hoi (the Vietnamese Independence League) or Viet Minh, was founded; it was committed to ridding Vietnam of both the French and the Japanese invaders. Its leaders, Ho Chi Minh and Vo Nguyen Giap, were now to shape the course of Vietnam's history.

Ho Chi Minh in 1957. Ho, the founder and leader of the Democratic Republic of Vietnam, was the inspiration for many to struggle for Vietnam's independence.

Ho Chi Minh's real name was Nguyen That Than; Ho Chi Minh was one of his many aliases. It was chosen by Ho and means "He who enlightens".

Early contacts with America

In order to gather information about the Japanese, to harass them and to give support to US agents in the region, the Americans had already established intelligence-gathering centres – OSS (Office of Strategic Services) bases – in China. They had the co-operation of Mao Tse-tung and the Chinese

32

Communists and of the Chinese Nationalists led by Chiang Kai-shek. In 1945 they began to look more closely at what was going on in Indo-China. The Viet Minh were well-placed to help.

In 1943 American OSS contact with the Chinese Nationalists had enabled them to obtain the release of Ho, who had been imprisoned on suspicion of being a communist agent. In return for this, Ho provided the Americans with information on Japanese bases and troop movements. He asked for arms which, at first, the OSS refused to provide. By 1945 the Americans were supplying and training the Viet Minh, little realizing that the techniques they were teaching would one day be used against them.

Military co-operation between the Viet Minh and the American OSS to hasten the defeat of the Japanese was regarded with great suspicion by the French. They were fearful that the Viet Minh would gain control of the Vietnamese countryside. With arms and equipment provided by the Americans the Viet Minh set up a base at Tan Trao where Ho was later to establish his provisional government.

The Democratic Republic of Vietnam

The end of the war against Japan came suddenly with the dropping of atomic bombs on Hiroshima and Nagasaki. The French now wished to regain control of their colonies in Indo-China. In Vietnam they would have to contend with the Viet Minh, for Ho Chi Minh was established in the village region of Tan Trao and Viet Minh officials were already in command of Hanoi. From Tan Trao, on 25th August, 1945, Ho Chi Minh announced the establishment of the Democratic Republic of Vietnam (DRV) but remaining within the French colonies with which its future relations would have to be negotiated. 2nd September was chosen by Ho as the official Independence Day for Vietnam. True independence was still a long way off.

The United States supports France

The Americans would not recognize the DRV, despite Ho's co-operation with the OSS against the Japanese, and despite the fact that Vietnam's Declaration of Independence copied that of the United States: "All men are created equal. They are endowed by their Creator with certain inalienable rights, among these are Life, Liberty and the pursuit of Happiness." In 1945-46 Ho Chi Minh (as the *Pentagon Papers* showed) repeatedly asked the US government for recognition. Without it, relations between the Viet Minh and the French degenerated into hostility, then war.

US President Franklin Roosevelt had written earlier: "France has had the country [Vietnam], thirty million inhabitants, for nearly one hundred years, and the people are worse off than they were at the beginning." It looked as though the US would support the end of French colonialism. However, after the Second World War, American fears about the rise of the Soviet Union grew. With the beginning of the "Cold War" and especially after the establishment of a Communist government in China in 1949, the United States gave its support in Vietnam to France. Ho Chi Minh was forced back into the countryside of North Vietnam from where a guerrilla war was fought against the French.

The guerrilla war against the French

On 20th December, 1946, Ho Chi Minh broadcast a call for a war of national resistance against the French, as his troops, led by General Giap, established bases close to the Chinese border. Thousands of French troops were unable to find Ho Chi Minh and the Viet Minh who, changing camps almost daily, kept up an unrelenting pressure against them. The Viet Minh, using the example of Mao Tse-tung in China, moved

Ho Chi Minh directs the Viet Minh in their campaign against the French.

and worked among the people like fish in water. By 1947 the Viet Minh could count upon a million supporters from a variety of organizations representing peasants, workers, women, youth and even religious groups. Throughout the North self-defence units had been organized in every village, street and factory. These units preceded the building of a regular army. The Viet Minh had eyes and ears everywhere and were able to strike at any time. The conventional forces of the French were all but useless against them.

American aid The Viet Minh attack on the French began in earnest in 1950. Ho Chi Minh had been recognized as Vietnam's leader by Mao Tse-tung, now head of the new Communist government in China, and by the Soviet government. In response, the French increased their demands to the United States for assistance. When the Korean war began in June 1950 the US government granted $10 million of artillery aid to the French, who by 1954 were receiving more than $1,000 million aid and were spending in Indo-China as much as had been given to France in the Marshall Plans for reconstruction after World War II.

The vast expenditure by the United States was to make no difference to the eventual result of the war. The Viet Minh had a considerable advantage over the French in mobile forces and, with Chinese equipment, were over-running French bases in the North. In France the war became thoroughly unpopular, dividing the nation, just as was to happen in the United States. Thousands of troops had been killed and wounded, with nothing for France to show in return. Only massive defeat faced the French.

Dien Bien Phu Fear of "another Dien Bien Phu" was to haunt President Johnson during the siege of Khe Sanh in 1968 for it was at this village, called "the arena of the Gods", that the French were defeated and lost their Indo-Chinese empire.

Dien Bien Phu is a valley, close to the Laos border, surrounded by wooded hills. Control of it would have enabled the French to restrict Viet Minh supplies brought in from Laos. The French believed that the Viet Minh had no means of bringing weapons, food and supplies to fight a battle in this remote area. On 20th November, 1953, French parachutists began to land; a week later there were 10,000 in place, with a further 5,000 standing by. They confidently expected to be able to hold the base against any Viet Minh attack.

By December Ho Chi Minh and General Giap were

consolidating their forces. Food and supplies were brought to Dien Bien Phu from all over the country by every available means. "Iron Horses" (bicycles) were strengthened and adapted to carry sacks of rice enough to last the army several months. When the bicycle tyres burst, the Vietnamese tore their trousers into strips to strengthen the inner tubes. When close to the French they lived on cold food, for to light a fire would have given away their position. By January 1954 the French were completely encircled by the Viet Minh, unable to move in or out of the base, dependent upon supplies brought in from the air. They were outnumbered by three to one.

Ho Chi Minh described the situation to a foreign journalist. Taking off his straw helmet and turning it upside down on the table he felt in the bottom of it. "Dien Bien Phu is a valley, and it's completely surrounded by mountains. The cream of the French Corps are down there and we," he said, feeling the brim of the hat, "are around the mountains, and they'll never get out."

A soldier killed at Dien Bien Phu is carried away by a comrade.

General Giap began his offensive against the French on 12th March, 1954, using all 200 of his artillery. In the first hour 500 French troops died on one hill alone. French gunners were unable even to locate Giap's artillery. In the days that followed the outposts of the base at Dien Bien Phu were taken one by one by the Vietnamese. The French were forced into a smaller area, completely exposed to Vietnamese attackers. Each day the toll of dead and seriously wounded rose.

In Washington President Eisenhower drew up a plan to relieve the French: "Operation Vulture" would use three small nuclear bombs to destroy the Viet Minh. The plan was dropped because of opposition in Congress. By May 1954 the French commanders were daily expecting the Americans to help them. When they did not and when the Viet Minh stepped up their attacks, the French were forced to stop fighting. Now it was the Americans' turn in Vietnam.

A demoralized French Army is led away by the victorious Viet Minh in 1954.

How did the United States become involved in Vietnam? – 2 From 1954: Supporting the South

The Geneva Agreement

The Geneva Conference was held from 26th April to 21st July, 1954. It had been planned in January and February of that year by the American, British, French and Soviet foreign ministers, and "the problem of restoring peace in Indo-China" had been chosen at that time as an item for the agenda. Thus the Conference provided a way for the French to leave Vietnam after their defeat at Dien Bien Phu without too much loss of face.

By 1954 the Viet Minh were in control of more than three-quarters of Vietnam. Weary after years of fighting, they wanted to avoid prolonging the war with the French and risking drawing the US into the conflict. They were prepared, therefore, to make concessions.

The agreement that was signed in Geneva on 20th July, 1954, established the division of Vietnam into North and South at the 17th Parallel. This meant that the Viet Minh had to give up areas they controlled in the South, but they were prepared to do this since the agreement also provided for general elections leading to the unification of the country. They were confident of political victory in the elections and foresaw that Ho Chi Minh would be the leader of the unified Vietnam. Most observers also saw this as the most likely, and even desirable, outcome. But the idea was unacceptable to the US government of President Eisenhower, which disassociated itself from the agreement.

The growth of American involvement in the South

The agreement had divided Vietnam temporarily into the North, run by Ho Chi Minh and the Viet Minh, and the South, controlled by the regime of Bao Dai. Bao Dai was then replaced by Ngo Dinh Diem and for the next two years the US built up Diem's regime as "the best hope that we have in Vietnam". The Americans treated South Vietnam as a separate state and Diem, for his part, proclaimed the establishment of a "Republic of Vietnam", with himself as President, on 26th October, 1955.

The US was busy in Vietnam in other ways than supporting Diem. A psychological warfare operation with black propaganda leaflets claiming that "Christ has gone South" and "The Virgin Mary has departed from the North" resulted in the exodus from the North of almost 900,000 Vietnamese, mostly Catholics. This removed much needed management skills from the North, and at the same time provided Diem with very necessary support. Even so, these people provided a further element of instability to the South.

Diem refused to co-operate with Ho Chi Minh on the question of elections and unification. "We have not signed the Geneva Agreements," he claimed. "We are not bound in any way by these Agreements signed against the will of the Vietnamese people." In this he was encouraged by the United States.

Problems for the North

In the North the Viet Minh prepared for the elections and got on with the pressing task of economic development. It was an unfortunate fact of life that the area occupied by them in the North was much poorer than the rich agricultural land in the South. The North Vietnamese government in Hanoi maintained its commitment to the national elections but, even despite trying to reconvene the Geneva Conference, could make no progress in the face of the stone-walling of Diem and the Americans.

The formation of the National Liberation Front

From the late 1950s President Diem was under attack from forces within South Vietnam other than the Viet Minh. Diem's unpopularity came from his repressive policies. He jailed anyone who opposed French rule since to do so implied support for the Viet Minh. He alienated the peasants by his land reform, which raised rents and took away their control of local affairs.

By 1958 the National Front for the Liberation of Vietnam (NLF) had come into existence. It was to play a crucial role in the fight for independence and re-unification of Vietnam. The South Vietnamese government referred derisively to the NLF as "Viet Cong" and "Vietnamese Communists". In the countryside the peasants referred to them as "Viet Minh" even though, in the 1950s, NLF policies and demands were regarded *without* sympathy by the true Viet Minh in Hanoi. The NLF called for the overthrow of Diem and his replacement by a "broad national democratic coalition" and for the "election of a new National Assembly". Social and economic reforms and the withdrawal of all US military advisers were also included in the NLF's demands. The re-unification of Vietnam was to be a gradual process.

Clearly, the NLF was formed because of discontent and demands for change in the South. It was not formed as a result of pressure and encouragement from the Viet Minh. Yet the

Richard Nixon congratulates John Kennedy at his swearing in as President of the United States in 1960. Behind them stands Lyndon Johnson. Each was to be the President of the United States; each was to take the US deeper into the war until the final evacuation in 1975.

justification for the build-up of US Military, and for the escalation of the war to include bombardment of the North in the 1960s, was to be based upon the belief that the NLF *was* a creation of Hanoi.

The NLF fought actively against the South Vietnamese government and the US forces in the South. Therefore, naturally, they coordinated their actions with those of the Viet Minh whose military and political leaders had close, sometimes direct, contact with the South. But it was only in 1960 that the aims and strategy of the Viet Minh and the NLF came together in the formation of the National Liberation Front of South Vietnam.

President Kennedy John Kennedy became America's President in 1961, inheriting a number of policies from his predecessor Dwight Eisenhower. Among them was the conviction that the politics of South East Asia could be a danger to America's interests in the Pacific. Eisenhower told Kennedy of his "Domino Theory". If South Vietnam were to "fall" to the Viet Minh, the next dominoes to fall would be Laos, Cambodia and Burma. Eventually the falling dominoes would reach

Australia and New Zealand. Kennedy was, apparently, impressed by Eisenhower's fears. Certainly, from the start of his presidency, he was prepared to consider the use of US troops in Vietnam to support President Ngo Dinh Diem.

The build-up of Military in the South

In 1961 US helicopter pilots arrived in South Vietnam to lead the Southern troops. Within months they were flying into battle against the Viet Cong. The next year there were 10,000 US troops in Vietnam including 4,000 crack, anti-guerrilla

The first US military "advisers" in Vietnam were helicopter pilots who were soon fighting for the South. The importance of helicopters in the Vietnam War resulted in its being called "the Helicopter War".

forces, the Green Berets. American forces in Vietnam were to grow steadily in the 1960s: 2,000 in 1961; 10,000 in 1962; 14,000 in 1963; 16,500 in 1964; 53,500 in 1965; 267,000 in 1966. The figure was to reach nearly 550,000. During the same period the South Vietnamese army grew from 380,000 to 614,000. The number of Australian, New Zealand and Korean troops fighting alongside the Americans increased from 2,300 to 29,150.

The overthrow of President Diem

In May 1961 US Vice-President Lyndon Johnson had visited Saigon. On his return he described President Diem, whom he

41

had called the Winston Churchill of South East Asia, as having "admirable qualities" though being "remote from the people" and "surrounded by persons less admirable than he". Following this visit, and those of other advisers to the US President, the flow to Vietnam of military equipment, and of the men to fly and use it, had increased dramatically. A year later, despite the build-up of weaponry, the Viet Cong had taken the initiative. In fact, the Viet Cong had benefited more from the influx of US weapons than Diem's troops had, by capturing them in battle.

The optimism about Diem's policies evaporated in 1963 when he allowed vicious attacks on Buddhist monks who were protesting against religious persecution. Troops fired on a crowd showing a Buddhist flag in Hué, and in August 1963 Diem's troops attacked pagodas in Saigon, Hué and other cities. The response was a series of horrifying suicides by Buddhist monks who set fire to themselves on the streets of South Vietnam. When Diem resisted all US pressures to make concessions to the Buddhists, President Kennedy approved plans to overthrow him. Diem was ousted in a military coup in November 1963 and assassinated.

The Military was to play an important political role in South Vietnam from then on. A Junta of generals took over from Diem and in the next two years were replaced one after another in quick succession. Such instability had not been imagined by the American President who had agreed to Diem's overthrow.

Kennedy, like Diem, was himself to fall to assassin's bullets in November 1963.

President Johnson Within days of taking over as President from Kennedy, Lyndon B. Johnson announced that US military support to South Vietnam would continue. It is an irony of history that Johnson, who in 1954 had blocked the use of atomic weapons against the Viet Minh at Dien Bien Phu, was now involved in escalating the war even to a point, at Khe Sanh, where he himself would consider using nuclear weapons. Vietnam was to be the albatross around Johnson's neck for the whole of his presidency. It would rob him of the resources to deal with pressing social issues at home, so that he could not build the "Great Society" he had worked as a politician to bring about. Johnson had campaigned against American military involvement in Vietnam. Now, as President, he was trapped by the role of world policeman which Eisenhower and Kennedy before him had taken on.

Why did the United States lose the war?

During the 1960s the US employed more and more sophisticated weapons in Vietnam and yet still did not defeat the Vietnamese. How did the North Vietnamese fight back?

This US Army poster sums up how many American soldiers were made to see their role in Vietnam. Unfortunately, the "enemy" which they went on to identify in Vietnam was almost everyone around them.

The possibility of bombing the North By 1964 President Johnson had plans at his disposal for massive air attacks on North Vietnam. A more aggressive Commander, General William Westmoreland, controlled US forces in Vietnam (still called "advisory"), and covert attacks on the North Vietnamese were on the increase in retaliation for the successes of the Viet Cong in the South. Unknown to the rest of the world, the US was also involved in secret bombing of Laos, and the Laotian border with Vietnam. President Johnson was of the opinion that bombing North Vietnam would bring Ho Chi Minh to the conference table, but before letting the bombing go ahead wanted to initiate a dialogue with Hanoi.

In June 1964 a Canadian intermediary in Hanoi met with Pham Van Dong, one of the founders of the Viet Minh and a close aide and friend of Ho Chi Minh. He had nothing to offer the Vietnamese, only passed on the information that American patience was "growing extremely thin" and that the US, if pushed, might carry the war to the North. Pham Van Dong explained the North's position: they wanted peaceful re-unification of their country and negotiations to bring that about. But they were in no hurry and would wait until the South was ready, even if this were difficult for the United States. "The US," he said, "can go on increasing aid to South Vietnam. It can increase its own army personnel. I suffer to see the war go on, develop, intensify. Yet our people are determined to struggle. It is impossible for Westerners to understand the force of the people's will to resist, and to continue. The struggle of our people exceeds the imagination. It has astounded us, too." He went on to say that what was occurring in Vietnam was a war to the end, which was unwinnable for the United States, and that the North would not provoke the United States into any escalation of the war. That was to come, however, within weeks of the conversation.

The Gulf of Tonkin incident On 2nd August, 1964, a US Navy destroyer, the USS *Maddox*, was collecting intelligence information off the coast of North Vietnam in the Gulf of Tonkin. The captain signalled that his ship was under attack from North Vietnamese torpedo boats whilst in international waters. Two days earlier there had been a covert South Vietnamese attack on the North Vietnamese coast, in which US "advisers" had been involved. President Johnson ordered another destroyer to the assistance of the *Maddox*. When this too was "attacked" – and there is considerable doubt whether a second "attack" did, in fact, take place – the President called for retaliatory air strikes against North Vietnam. On 5th August, in a raid that lasted just ten minutes, oil and port facilities were bombed, destroying ten per cent of the North's oil supplies.

The US Congress had supported Johnson's action against the North and, in so doing, had given him a "blank cheque" to wage war on the Vietnamese. It was a decision that was to cause much regret and bitterness as the war continued.

US bombing of North Vietnam resulted in great loss of life and material damage. In 1986, without substantial aid, the Vietnamese were still coping with the destruction.

The reality of bombing the North

Bombing of the North was stepped up in 1965 after a Viet Cong attack on the US military base at Pleiku. On 2nd March waves of fighter-bombers devastated roads, bridges, railway-lines and ports. Reporting the raids on television, President Johnson said: "I regret the necessities of war have compelled us to bomb North Vietnam. We have carefully limited these raids. They have been directed at concrete and steel and not at human life."

45

"Rolling Thunder", the name given to the bombing offensive, was designed to hit the North in waves and to "bring the North to its knees within a few months". The bombing continued for eight years, during which time 350,000 bombing raids occurred, dropping eight million tons of bombs, four times the tonnage used in World War II. In addition to concrete and steel being hit, hundreds of thousands of Vietnamese were killed, together with 8,000 US airmen.

US intelligence had under-estimated the North's defences and resources to strike back. When the "Rolling Thunder" offensive did not bring the North to its knees but, as became clear, actually hardened North Vietnamese resolve, there was no alternative but for land forces to be rushed into the fight. The first US combat forces landed in the North shortly after the bombing began.

Helicopters were a crucial piece of American weaponry in the Vietnam war, able quickly to move troops in and out of battle areas.

Helicopters and bombers Even with the build-up of land forces, the use of planes and helicopters was crucial to the way the Vietnam war was

All forms of transport were used to supply and equip the Viet Cong fighting in South Vietnam.

fought. Helicopters gave US forces undreamed-of mobility. Whole battalions of troops could be lifted into the battle-field for surprise operations against the Viet Cong. US helicopters were equipped with awesome weapons: M50 machine guns that fired thousands of rounds of bullets per minute and rockets that could strike targets half a mile away. Often these were used indiscriminately against "the enemy", more often

47

than not meaning Vietnamese peasants trying to carry on their lives in the midst of the war. Many bomber pilots owe their lives to the rescue helicopters, the "Jolly Green Giants", which picked up crashed pilots often within the North. Two hundred were rescued from the North in this way.

Most pilots were not rescued. The United States lost 3,720 planes in the North and South to Viet Cong artillery, rocket and anti-aircraft fire, at a cost of more than $5,000 million. Five thousand helicopter pilots were killed; and five thousand bomber and fighter pilots. The chance of crashing and being captured was so high that all pilots carried a card which read: "I am an American. I need your assistance. My Government will repay you."

President Johnson believed that an air war would be more

A captured B52 pilot. Despite the potential to "bomb Vietnam back to the stone age", massive bombing did not shift the war in America's favour.

acceptable politically than a ground war as air war implied that the fighting could take place "at a distance", with less chance of US casualties. He was also confident that air attacks would bring the North to negotiations. But his air war of a few months lasted for many years and although the most sophisticated and destructive weapons were used against them, the North Vietnamese continued to advance on the South.

Vietnam was used as a test-bed for high-technology weaponry. Satellites scanned the terrain, laser-guided bombs were developed, electronic sensors left in jungles and alongside trails used by the Viet Cong relayed information of troop movements, and devices that could "smell" people below them were flown across Vietnam to hunt out Viet Cong guerrillas.

President Johnson personally selected targets and weapons to be used, each Tuesday lunchtime at a special White House meeting. His most destructive weapon was the B52 bomber, half as long as a football field, and which was capable of raining down 37 tons of bombs from six miles above the ground. These bombers flew unseen, unheard; their pilots, guided to the targets by radar and computer, were unaware of what they were actually destroying. Each bomb dropped caused a quarter-mile-wide area of destruction. Flying so high, the B52s were not as vulnerable to missile attack as fighter bombers flying at lower altitudes. But B52s were destroyed by SAMs (surface-to-air missiles) and their pilots were captured.

The North Vietnamese response   The North Vietnamese had a range of weapons, provided by the Soviet Union and China, to use against air attacks. But their main weapon was their mobility. Hanoi was evacuated

The bombing of the North led to the construction outside towns and cities of tunnels in which children went to school and workshops were set up.

Hanoi's children never left home without straw headgear to protect them from the bombing. Shelters were dug at the side of roads to give protection during bombing raids.

to the countryside once it became a US target. Only people essential to the war remained in the city; the rest went to the country where entire villages had already developed systems of underground tunnels in which people lived and worked, safe from the bombing. In Hanoi and the other cities of the North concrete bomb shelters were built on every street. All North Vietnamese children carried woven straw protective helmets. Despite the massive US bombing, which caused enormous destruction and many civilian casualties, the North continued to rebuild and to advance.

Fighting the Viet Cong The air war failed against the North largely because the Vietnam war was a guerrilla war which the US mistakenly treated as a conventional war. Viet Cong rifle fire was capable of bringing down costly and sophisticated US planes and helicopters, and simple techniques of warfare were devastatingly effective on the ground. By 1965, according to CIA reports, the Viet Cong controlled at least 50 per cent of the countryside in the South. Their success was due to their appeals to nationalism and to their efficient political organization. Such control by the Viet Cong was obviously a threat to the US and the government in the South. Throughout the 1960s they looked for ways to influence the country people and to wean them away from the Viet Cong.

Instead of demoralizing the people of North Vietnam, the US bombing served only to inspire them to continue the fight for independence. (From a coloured woodcut.)

We will fight and fight from this generation to the next

In the early 1960s the United States began its "Strategic Hamlets" programme. Whole village communities were relocated to fortified "hamlets". The idea was to remove the inhabitants from the influence of the Viet Cong, prevent them from providing supplies to the Viet Cong and "protect" them from what the Viet Cong might do to them. In the same way the French had set up "Agrovilles" during their war in Vietnam, to keep the country people away from the influence of the Viet Minh. The "Strategic Hamlets" programme was one of the most unpopular moves of the United States. Country people became embittered as they were wrenched from the homes and land that had long been held by their families.

Nor were the elaborate social services available as promised to those resettled, for the funds had been siphoned off by corrupt officials. Adequate compensation for the move was rarely given since this money, too, was appropriated by South Vietnamese involved in the programme. The Viet Minh described the "Strategic Hamlets" as "camouflaged concentration camps".

When the "Strategic Hamlets" programme failed, the

Americans began bombing and rocket raids and artillery and helicopter assaults on any village in the South which they suspected of having connections with the Viet Cong. Great violence was shown to the country people. When the Americans realized that the brutal treatment was making the South Vietnamese *more* sympathetic to the Viet Cong, they sought other ways of winning them over.

A programme of "pacification" began in 1968, to win the "hearts and minds" of the South Vietnamese people through displays of goodwill. $1,700 million was ear-marked to provide "carrots" in place of "sticks". Thousands of tons of high-yield rice seed were distributed, along with thousands of tons of soya beans, gallons of cooking oil, tons of fertilizer, building materials and consumer goods. A nuclear reactor for the South was also available in the programme though never installed. The organizers of the programme soon lost heart

Destruction of the homes of Viet Cong suspects was a common part of the war in the countryside of South Vietnam.

when no immediate winning-over of the people occurred. The US resorted to a harsher plan.

"Operation Phoenix" worked through fear. It was designed to capture or eliminate the Viet Cong's most important activists in the South. Anyone suspected of involvement with the Viet Cong would be imprisoned. Thousands were, and few were given their freedom again. Torture was routine in interrogations: in one case a woman suspect was starved to death; another suspected Viet Cong had a metal rod tapped through his ear into his brain. B52s would flatten the village, killing everyone in it, of anyone suspected of being a Viet Cong activist. 30,000 people were killed as a result of "Operation Phoenix". That the Viet Cong had been dealt a blow was shown by the fact that after 1972 the North deployed more regular troops in the South.

Weapons used in the war on the ground

The North Vietnamese and the Viet Cong in the South fought the best-equipped army in the world. In fact, the US ground forces probably carried far more equipment than was

Simple techniques like rifle fire to bring down US bombers and helicopters were devastatingly effective in the hands of the Viet Cong and defence groups in the North. (A sketch entitled "Everyone ready for action".)

The Viet Cong fighting in the South, as this cartoon shows, used both simple, home-made weapons and sophisticated weaponry captured from the South Vietnamese and American troops.

necessary. The Vietnamese had no ships to use against the US seventh fleet which could bombard the country from the South China Sea, striking six miles inland. Nor did they have any shore batteries with which to attack US warships.

The Vietnamese were dependent upon supplies from the Soviet Union and China and, in the ground war, these were more than a match for the US weaponry. Much of their equipment, like the AK47 rifle and the B40 rocket launcher, was more accurate and reliable than comparable US weapons. Even small arms fire could bring down American planes.

A good deal of the North Vietnamese arsenal was home-made. The Viet Cong would capture US weapons in raids and make new ones from the shells and bombs they had obtained. The steel casing of bombs and shells would be cut, the explosives removed and the metal used for making road mines. Many of these weapons were especially feared by US troops. For example, "Bouncing Betty" was a mine which jumped in the air before exploding; and "toe-poppers" were small mines which were capable of taking off a foot or a heel of anyone who stepped on one. Unexploded anti-personnel bombs, specially designed by the US for the Vietnam war, were often used by the Viet Cong against the Americans themselves. Traps made of sharpened stakes were another feared weapon of the Viet Cong.

Napalm is a sticky, phosphorus-based burning material which was extensively used by the US against the Viet Cong. Photographs of children killed and maimed by napalm bombs provoked outrage throughout the world and did much to generate international support for Ho Chi Minh and the Viet Cong.

The deciding factor Finally, whilst the Viet Cong remained dedicated to their cause, US troops were demoralized, not wishing to be the last to die in Vietnam in what had become identified as an unwinnable, unpopular war. The fight had gone out of US troops after the Tet Offensive of 1968 and the support of the American people for the war was also lost. US forces, despite their overwhelming military capability, were not fighting a war in which they had any commitment other than following orders. As Pham Van Dong had prophesied, it was "a war to the end, which the United States won't win in any event".

Throughout the world people were horrified by this image of young children burned by napalm dropped on their village.

What was the cost of the war?

American casualties   Fifty-seven thousand Americans and two million Vietnamese died in the war. Had the same proportion of the American population been killed as was the case for Vietnam, there would have been 10 million American dead. 150,000 Americans returned home on stretchers after receiving horrible injuries; a further half million returned with emotional problems. Many felt angered that their sacrifice and service in Vietnam were not properly recognized. There was no victory parade as there had been after World War II. But there was no victory to celebrate. By the 1970s there was little sympathy left for the war and American people did not want to be reminded of it since it had cost so many lives and caused so much division and anger at home. For the Vietnam veterans this was difficult to accept and they protested at the way society shunned them. Not until 1985, ten years after the final withdrawal from Vietnam, was a memorial erected in Washington to the dead of America's longest war.

Families who had lost sons, brothers, daughters, husbands, fathers, wives and mothers were further casualties of the war. Those who received disabled members back into their family suffered too. The "Vietnam Syndrome" affected many who returned. They had spent years in Vietnam regarding their enemy as "Charlie" or "Gooks" or "Slants"; they had been deliberately kept from seeing the enemy as human beings, flesh and blood like themselves. Once home, many Americans realized the enormity of their crimes in Vietnam, that what they had done was no way to treat a nation, bombing, burning and taking what they wanted from the people. Such was the extent of feelings like this that a programme of psychiatric care had to be developed to deal with problems resulting from the war. For a hard core of veterans no psychiatric help could cure their anger, frustration and alienation from society. They were unable to relate to other people and took to the woods to live off the land, killing animals for food as they had been taught to do in the jungles of Vietnam.

After the war in Vietnam   At Tet, the Vietnamese New Year, the two million dead of the war are remembered, and at noon every day in Hanoi remembrance chimes ring out across the city. The North

Vietnamese were not demoralized by the war as the Americans had been. They had been fighting a war for the freedom and independence of their country and when that was achieved, in 1975, there was cause for rejoicing as well as for rebuilding. In the South, whose government had been corrupt, and where many had become used to the American way of life, people were afraid of the unification of Vietnam and of control by the North.

There was much to be done. The debris of the war, the wreckage of tanks and planes, was used for reconstructing factories, schools and other buildings. Those caught up in the old regime in the South were forced to work in rural areas. North and South were reunited as the Socialist Republic of Vietnam. From outside, aid came from the Soviet Union, Scandinavia and Australia. The United States was the only major country not to recognize the new Vietnam. Nor did the US provide any aid for reconstruction despite promises to the contrary. There were, surely, compelling moral reasons why the United States should provide aid to the Socialist Republic of Vietnam?

The Vietnamese get on with the task of reconstruction after decades of war.

Agent Orange As a result of handling defoliants like "Agent Orange", which were used against the Vietnamese, many Vietnam veterans in the United States have suffered illness and children born to them have been malformed. Americans have taken out law suits for damages because of this.

For ten years from 1962 at least 14 per cent of Vietnam's forests and 5 per cent of agricultural land were sprayed, sometimes more than once, with defoliants killing off all plant life. In some parts of the country trees and plants have never grown again. The intention was to remove the cover under which the Viet Cong could operate and, at the same time, to hit at food resources. 44 million litres of "Agent Orange" were dropped on Vietnam, 20 million litres of "Agent White" and 8 million units of "Agent Blue"; all are toxic herbicides of which "Agent Orange" is the worst since it contains Dioxin, a very dangerous poison.

The chemical warfare on Vietnam has resulted in the pollution of the whole countryside with potentially dangerous consequences for the entire population. There has been a rise in the numbers of cancers caused by exposure to herbicides, and medical studies in Vietnam have also shown genetic abnormalities similar to those seen in Japan, resulting from exposure to radiation. All the indications are that there has been a long-term health effect on those exposed to the herbicides in Vietnam.

The "boat people" Material damage was not the only result of the war in Vietnam. In April 1975, in the South alone, there were a million widows and 800,000 orphans and children abandoned by their, largely American, soldier fathers. Hundreds of thousands of people had been uprooted. In Saigon, the 300,000 "traders" who had serviced the Americans and the privileged in the South suddenly found themselves redundant. Many fled, if they had the chance, in the airlift that facilitated the Americans' withdrawal in April 1975. Stories that there would be a bloodbath when the Viet Cong forces took Saigon added to the panic of those days. Between 1975 and 1978 a further trickle of refugees was allowed by the Vietnamese government.

In 1978, when the government restricted the trading activities of the Hoa, the Chinese community in Vietnam, many of these people decided to leave for China and other countries where there were already large Hoa communities. The refugees were dubbed "boat people" as they arrived in crowded ships. Their exodus from Vietnam was accompanied by an anti-Vietnam campaign in the world's press. The Vietnamese government was accused of curtailing human rights, yet the great majority who left Vietnam did so for economic reasons. They were not only large traders unable to stand the privations of reconstruction but also, often, employees such as bar workers whose skills were no longer in demand. The Vietnamese government is not opposed to people leaving the country if they have entry into other countries where members of their family are settled. It is opposed to illegal departures which could have an unsettling effect on the country.

Laos, Cambodia and China

The bombing and invasion of Cambodia and Laos, the countries close to Vietnam, were planned as soon as Richard Nixon became President. On his first day in office Richard Nixon asked the Pentagon chiefs how the US could "quarantine" Cambodia. Shortly after, the bombing of Cambodia began in secret. As bombing of North Vietnam decreased so bombing of Laos and Cambodia grew in intensity.

The secret bombing of Cambodia from 1969 let loose forces inside that country that were to have both brutal and tragic consequences. One of the first results was the overthrow in 1970 of Prince Sihanouk who had attempted to keep his country "neutral" and so avoid involvement in the war raging in Vietnam. His successor, Lon Nol, was supported by the US in the form of massive military aid. The aerial bombardment of Cambodia was followed by large-scale military operations on the ground, in search of Vietnamese bases. Ironically, the bases were pushed deeper into Cambodia, away from the border area, by the B52 bombing raids. The bombings and the land invasion of Cambodia created thousands of refugees. (The bombing of Laos and its invasion in 1971 was to have similar results.) By 1972 as many as two million Cambodians had been made homeless as a result of the war.

Fighting inside Cambodia between the pro-US forces of Lon Nol and the Communist Khmer Rouge added to Cambodia's tragedy. The real tragedy, however, began in April 1975 when the Khmer Rouge became the rulers. Cambodia (now named Kampuchea) became cut off from the outside world as her leaders attempted to establish a new society that began at the "Year Zero". The people of the capital, Phnom Penh, were forcibly evacuated to the countryside to a life of unrelenting toil. Anyone identified with the old regime, or with Vietnam, faced death in the most brutal fashion. Men, women and children were torn apart limb from limb. The most common form of execution, however, was beating to death with axe handles, since this saved ammunition. The agony of Kampuchea was compounded by the dislocation of the economy which resulted in starvation for hundreds of thousands of people. Between two and three million people died in Kampuchea from the Khmer Rouge purges, from illness and starvation.

Fighting between Vietnam and the Khmer Rouge began in 1976 and worsened in 1977, leading to a massive invasion by the Vietnamese in 1978. Some of the $15,000 million-worth of military materials left behind by the US were used by the Vietnamese. The Khmer Rouge were supported by China. In December 1978 the Vietnamese launched an invasion force to "liberate" Kampuchea and from that time they have left an occupation force there that has attempted to reconstruct Kampuchea from the ruins of the war. Visitors have noted the predominantly youthful population and the absence of old people.

Prince Sihanouk spoke forcefully about the destruction of his country to the writer William Shawcross:

> "There are only two men responsible for the tragedy in Cambodia, Mr Nixon and Dr Kissinger. Lon Nol was nothing without them and the Khmer Rouge were nothing without Lon Nol. By expanding the war into Cambodia, Nixon and Kissinger killed a lot of Americans and many other people, they spent enormous sums of money – $4 Billion and the results were the opposite of what they wanted. They demoralised America, they lost all of Indo China to the communists, and they created the Khmer Rouge." (*Side-Show: Kissinger, Nixon and the Destruction of Cambodia*, Fontana, 1980)

Ten years later The Vietnamese celebrated ten years of independence in Ho Chi Minh City in April 1985. The years since the fall of Saigon and the establishment of a unified country have been a period of reconstruction, diverted only by Vietnam's invasion of Kampuchea and China's invasion of Vietnam in 1979.

When the war ended there was an understandable desire to "leap forward" in rebuilding the country. The attempt to move too fast added to the tension within Vietnam that led to the exodus of the "boat people". After 1979 Vietnam's leaders opted for a more gradual pace of development, realizing that the laws of economic progress were quite different from the laws of war.

"The Lesson of Vietnam". Uncle Sam sits in a corner wearing a dunce's cap. What, if any, lessons were learned in the Vietnam War? In the 1980s many Americans thought the war in Vietnam could have been "won" if only it had been pursued more relentlessly.

Few countries have contributed to Vietnam's reconstruction. Sweden has built impressive health centres throughout the country; other western nations have preferred to work through the United Nations agencies. The Soviet Union has provided the most aid to Vietnam and is heavily involved in a variety of development projects. The United States has not given assistance since "destruction was mutual". The US has no trade with Vietnam, has given no aid nor reparation and has even blocked aid from other countries as well as development funds. In 1977, when India tried to send water buffaloes to Vietnam to replace those killed in the war (US pilots would often use water buffaloes for target practice), the US threatened to cancel India's own "food for peace" aid. A 1982 survey showed that more than seventy per cent of the US population still viewed the war not simply as a "mistake" but as "fundamentally wrong and immoral".

MIAs The US war in Indo-China ended with some 1,800 American servicemen listed as MIA (Missing in Action) in Vietnam, Laos and Cambodia. The uncertainty as to their fate resulted in stories in the press that prisoners remained in "enemy hands" after 1975. The Vietnamese government denied that American prisoners were being held in Vietnam and offered to investigate any evidence the US government had. Such cooperation between the two governments could lead to the re-establishment of economic and political relations, possibly even to the United States' giving the compensation and aid sought by the Vietnamese.

In both Vietnam and Laos excavations of crash sites have yielded the remains of US airmen who died in raids on the North. At a site near Hanoi in December 1985 American and Vietnamese officials dug out the remains of a B52 which had been destroyed by anti-aircraft missiles at about 8.30 p.m. on 20th December, 1972, during the "Christmas" raids on Hanoi and Haiphong. Some American families will know the fate of loved ones lost in Indo-China but it will be impossible to locate all those missing in action.

Further reading

Vietnam

General Van Tien Dung, *Our Great Spring Victory*, Monthly Review, 1977
Graham Greene, *The Quiet American*, Penguin, 1969
Michael Herr, *Dispatches*, Picador, 1978
Jean Lacouture, *Ho Chi Minh*, Allen Lane, 1968
New York Times, *The Pentagon Papers*, Bantam Books, 1971
Harrison Salisbury, *Behind the Lines – Hanoi*, Secker & Warburg, 1969
Frank Snepp, *Decent Interval*, Random House, 1977

Cambodia (Kampuchea)

William Shawcross, *Side-Show: Kissinger, Nixon and the Destruction of Cambodia*, Fontana, 1980

Laos

Arthur Dommen, *Conflict in Laos*, Praeger, 1964

Index